This book belongs to:

Excited for you to take a new approach to creating. We're all so used to coloring in the main subject of a coloring book or art piece. What if it was your job instead to color or create the background? Sounds fun right...

Choose your medium and get started putting the pieces together of what is happening in the background. Maybe you have lots of intricate details you want to draw with a pencil or black tip marker...or maybe you want to give a flowing and mesmerizing watercolor piece. Whatever you choose, have fun...pencils, watercolors, markers, crayons, pastels, acrylics, etc.

Be sure to let us know what you think leslietimm4@gmail.com and
don't forget to post or send some pictures so we can see all the great things being dreamed up.

Thanks for giving creativity a chance!

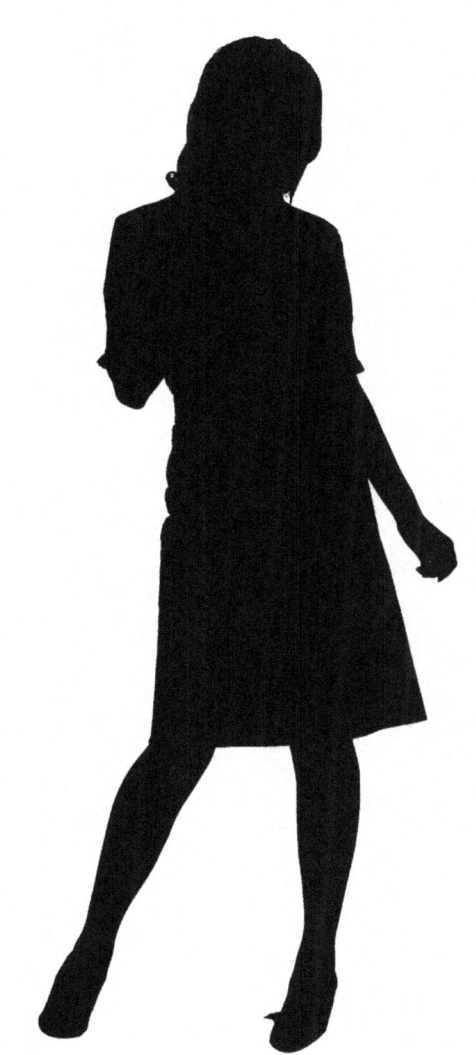

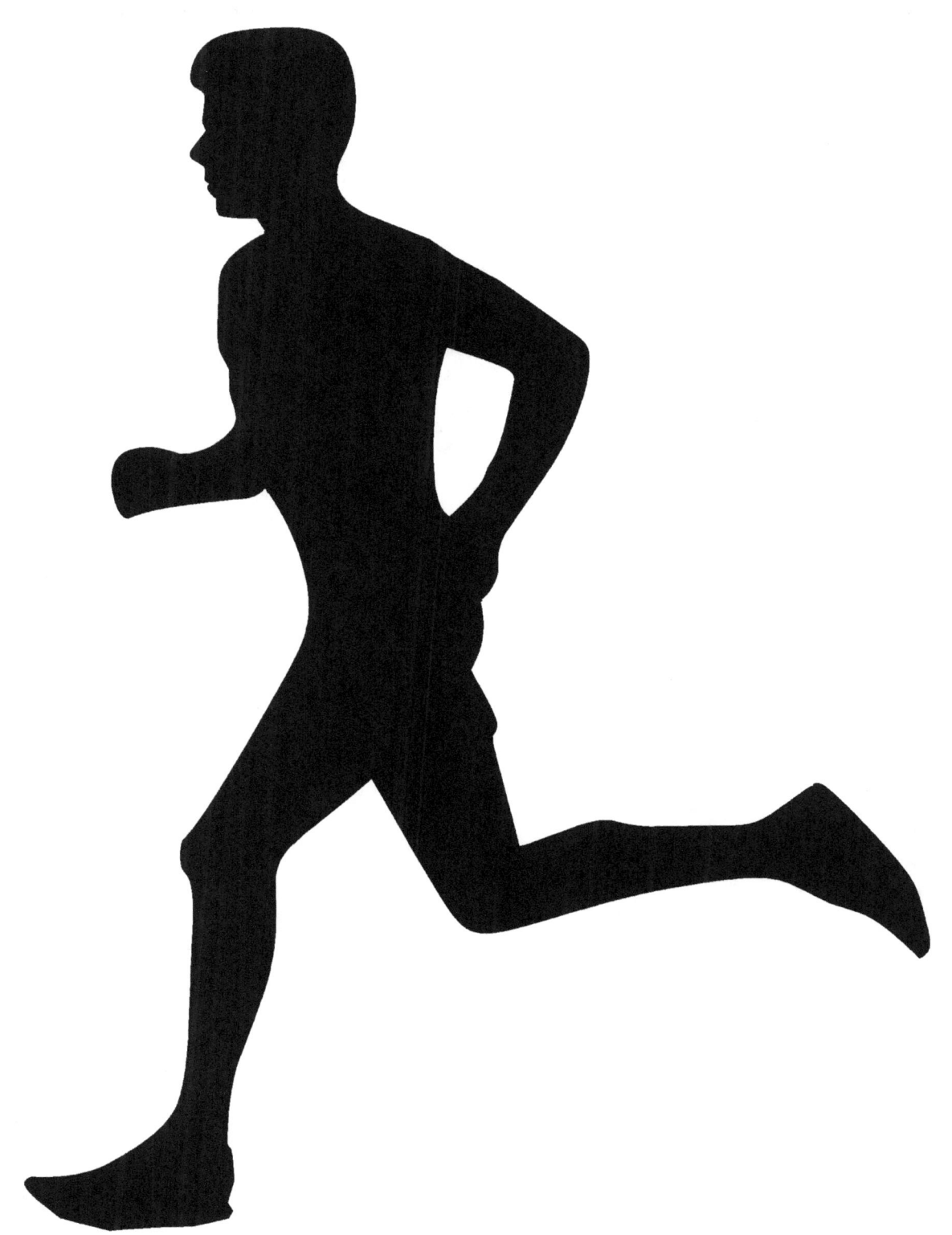

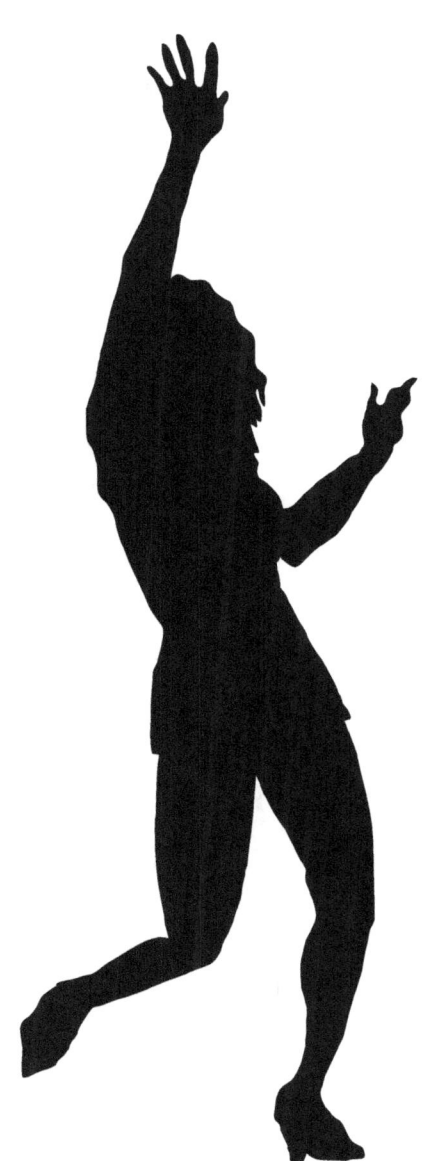

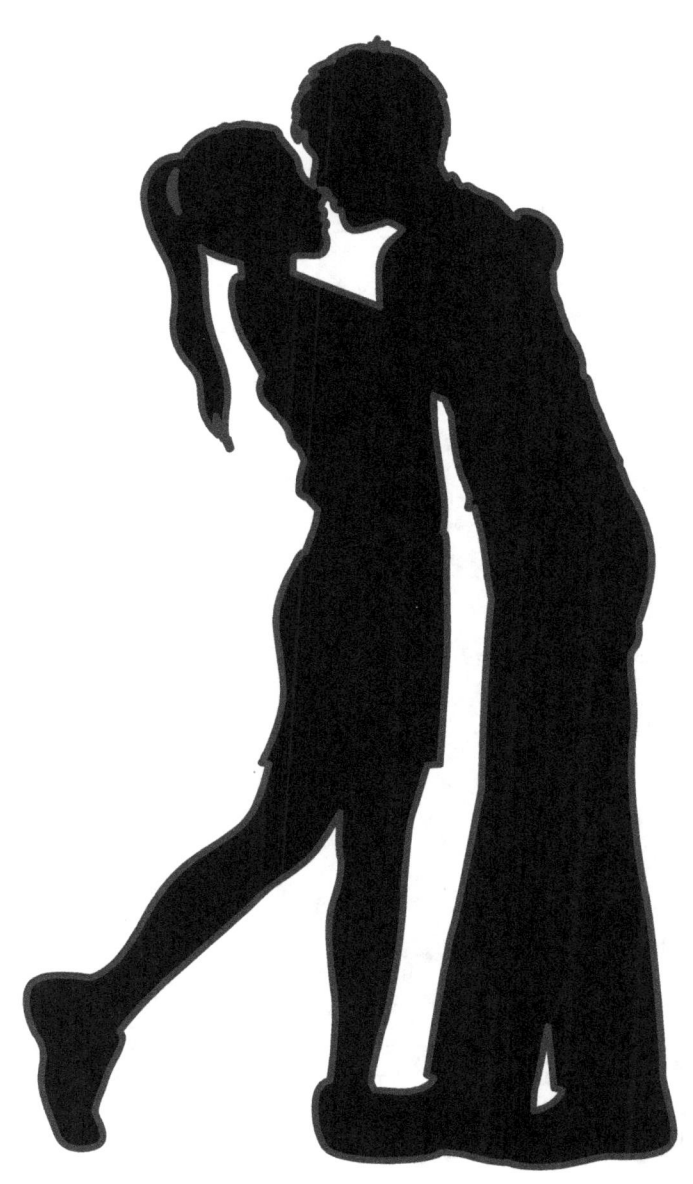

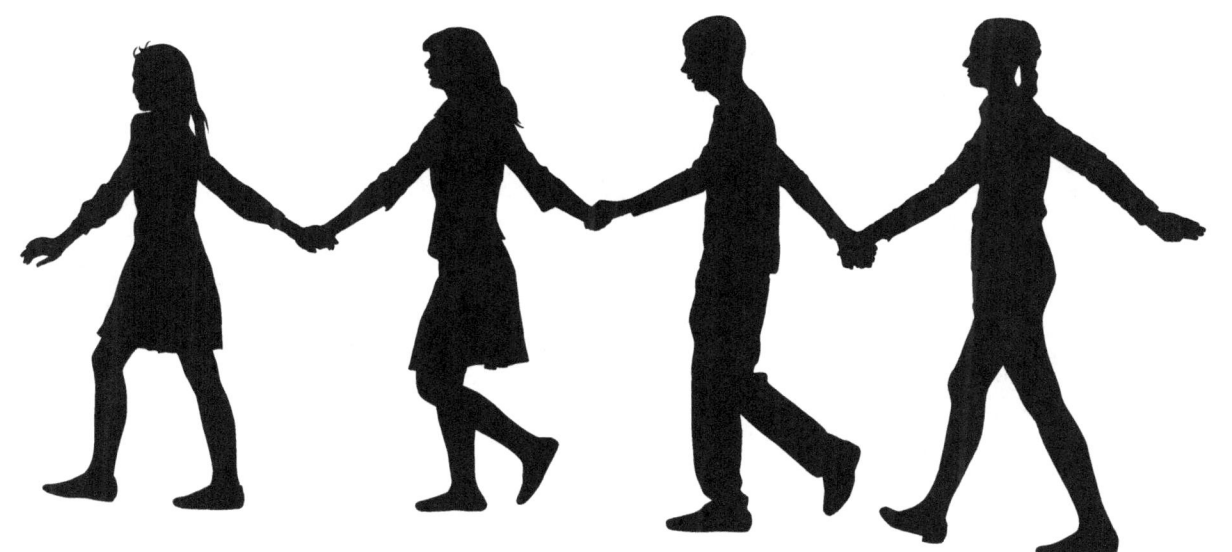

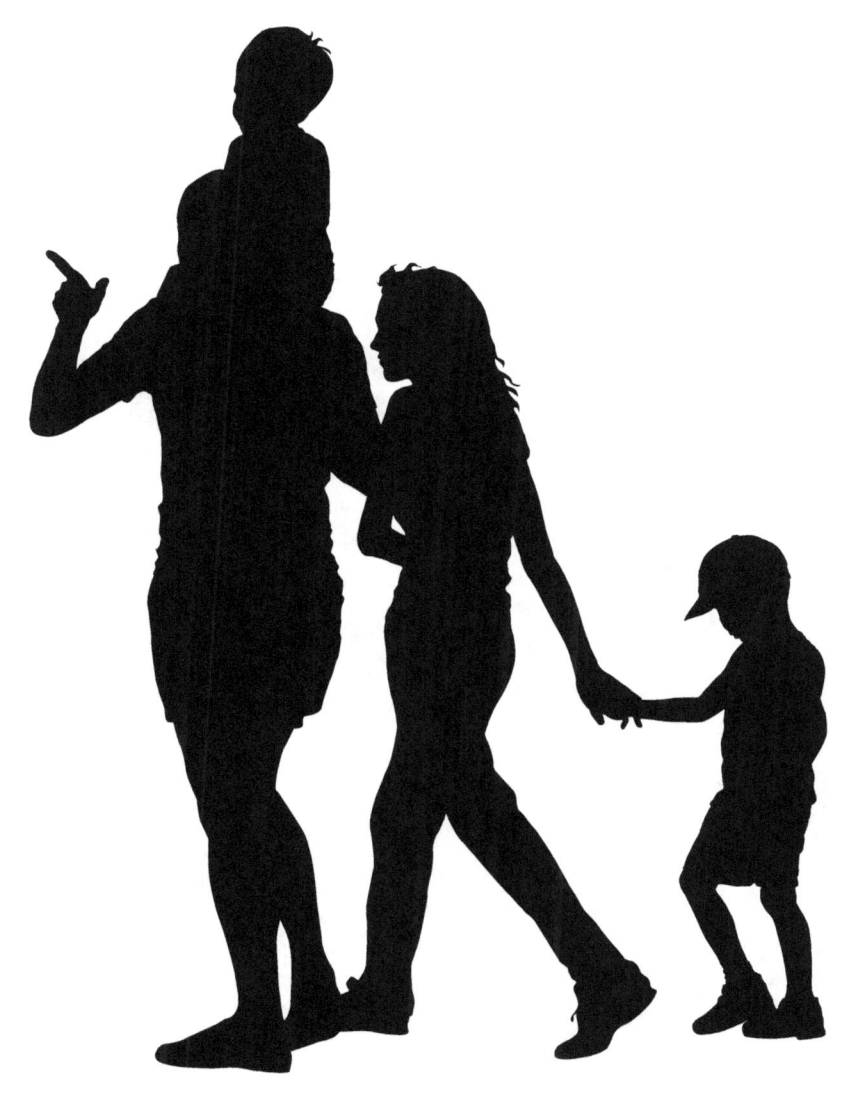

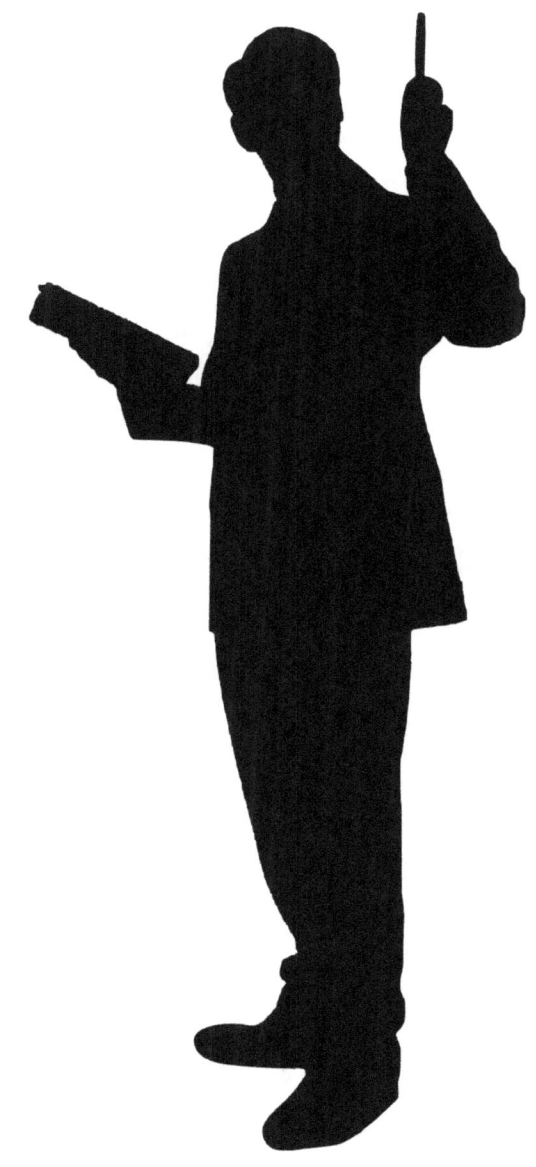

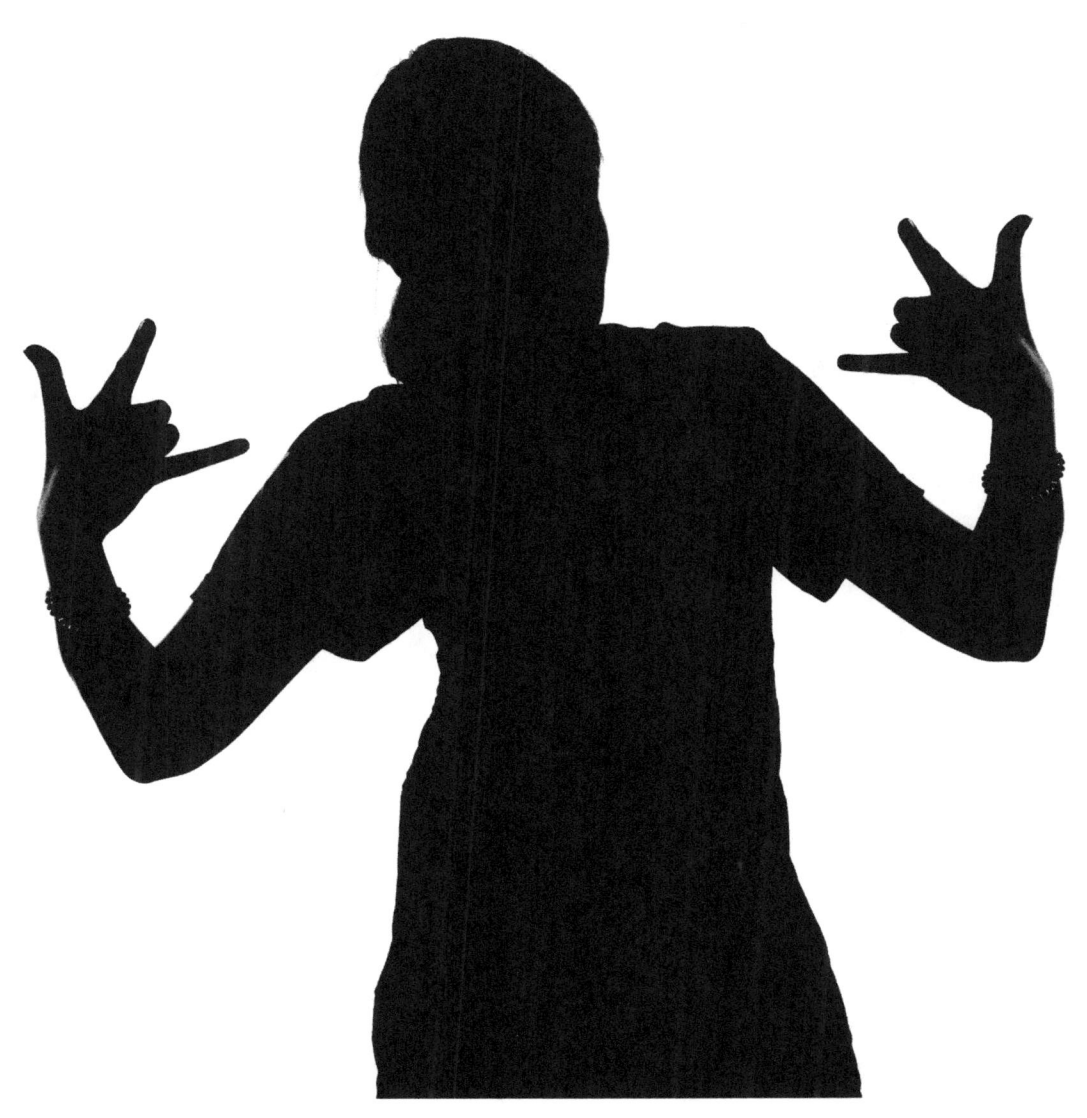

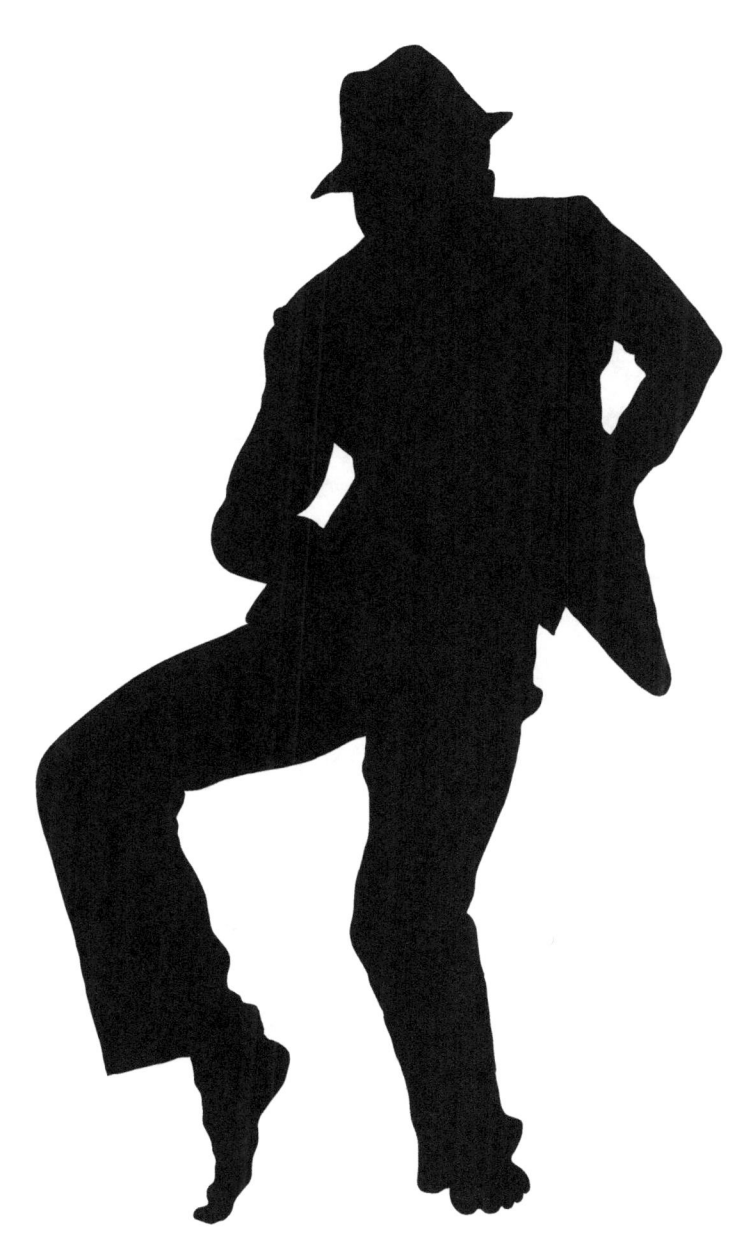

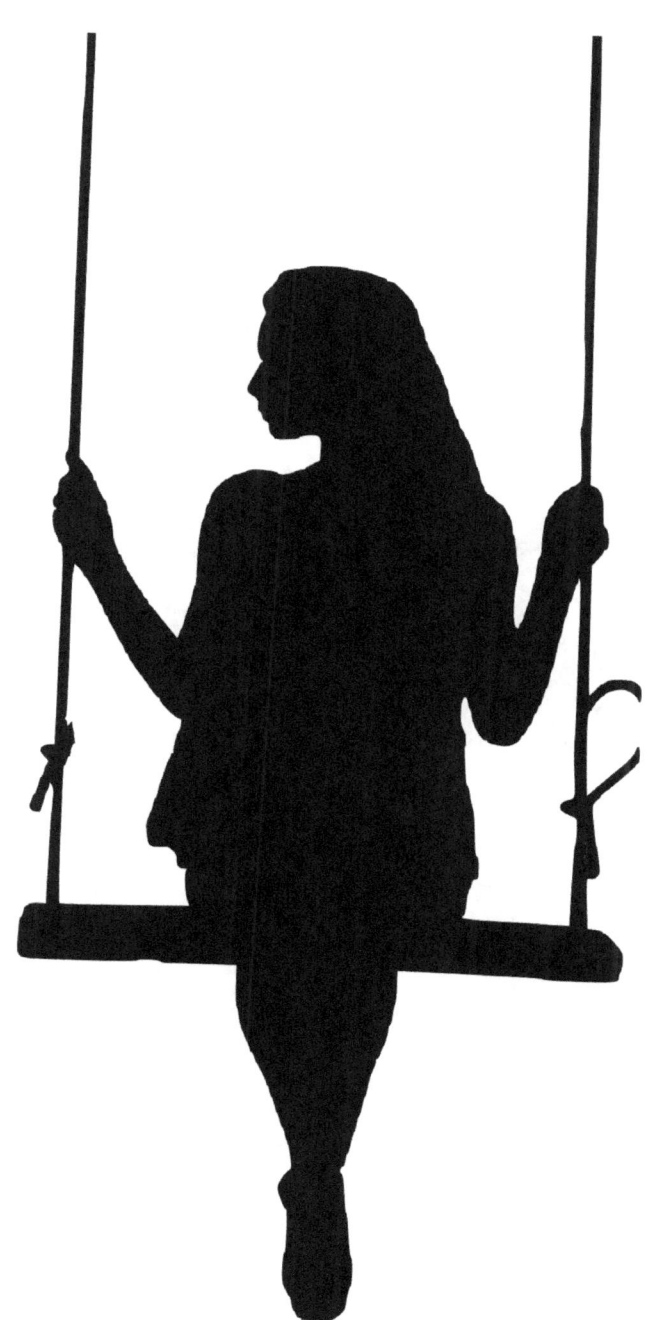

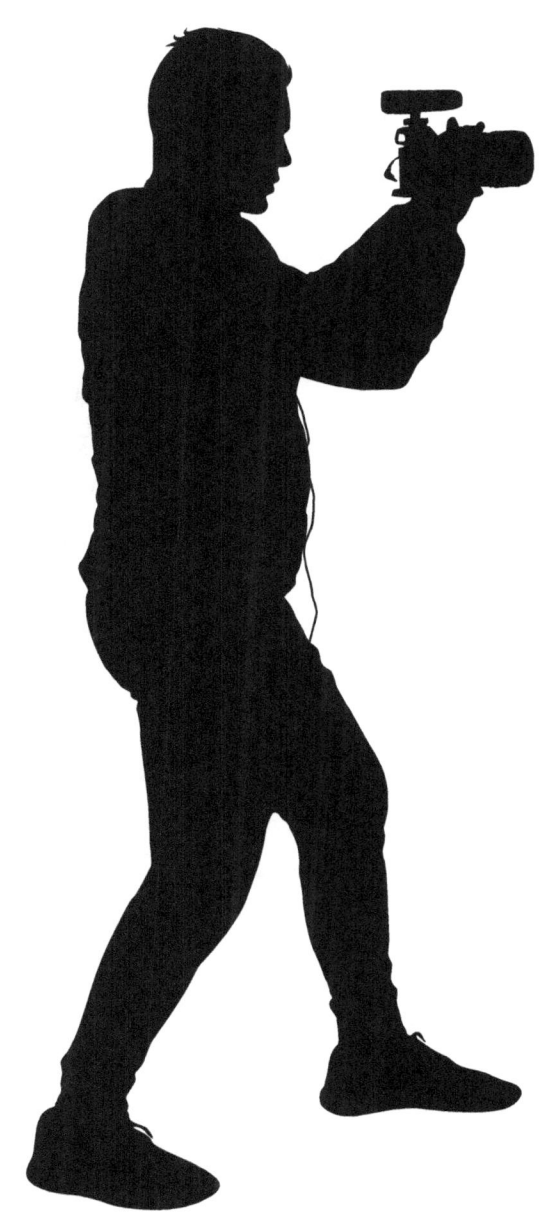

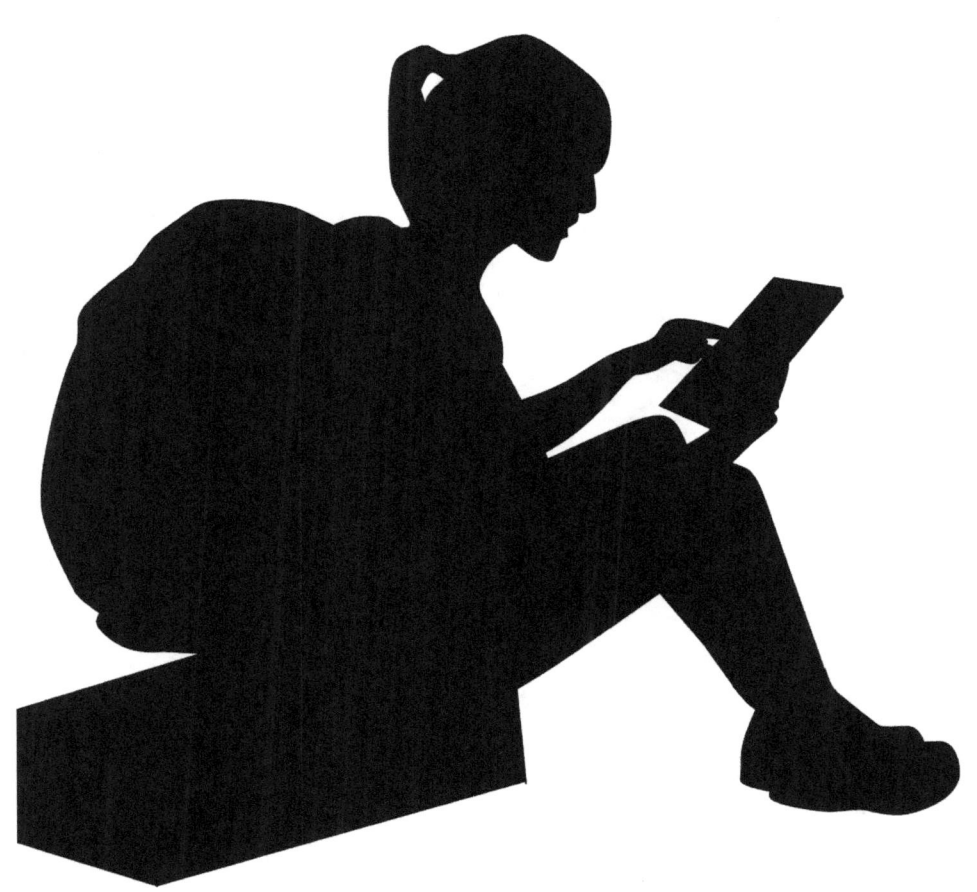

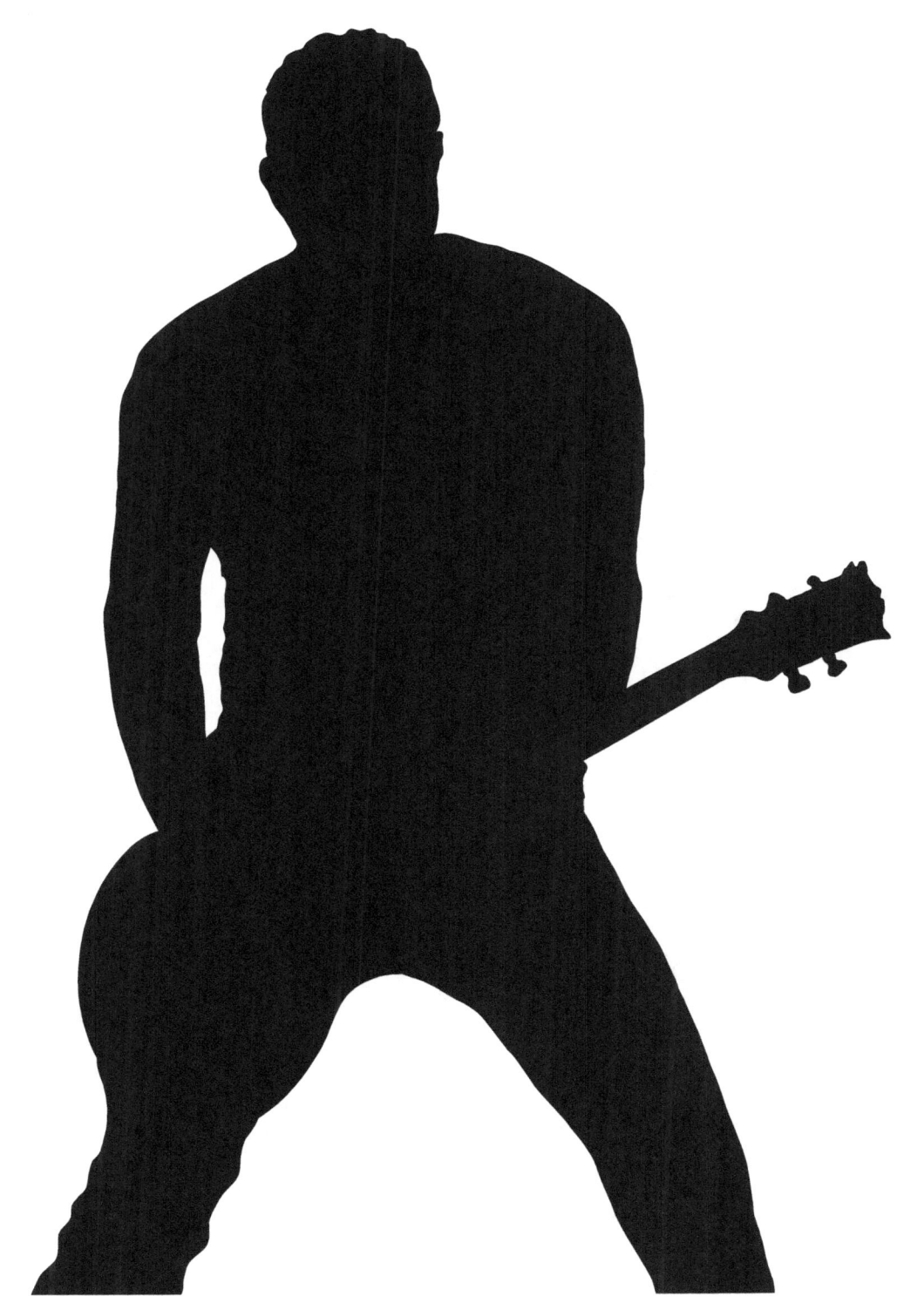

....

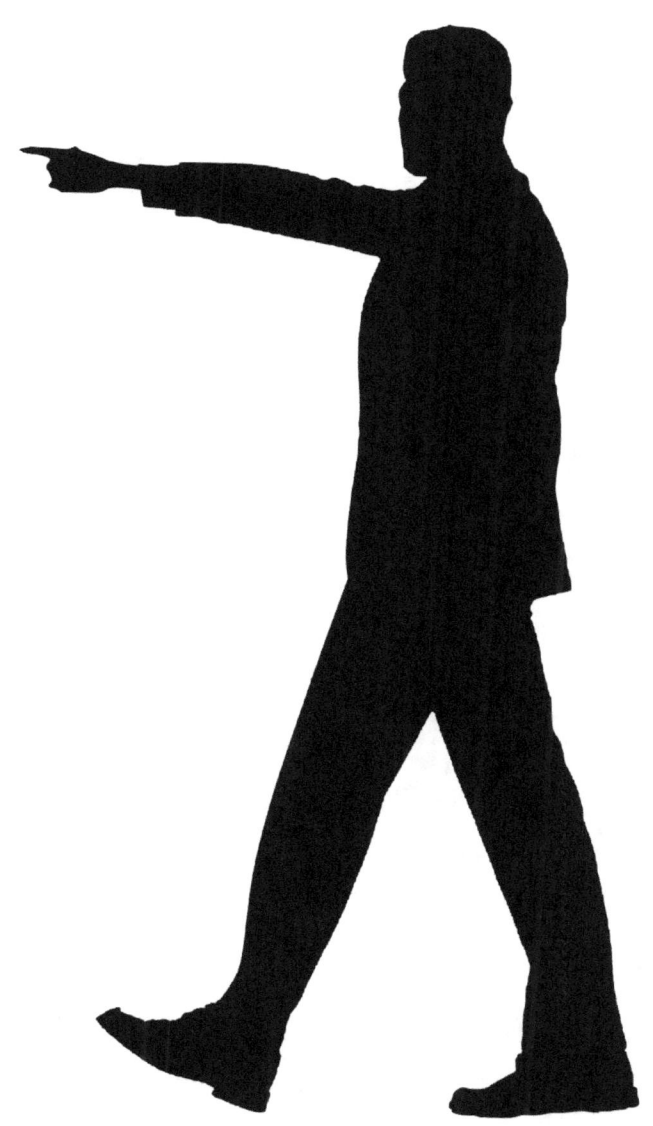

14

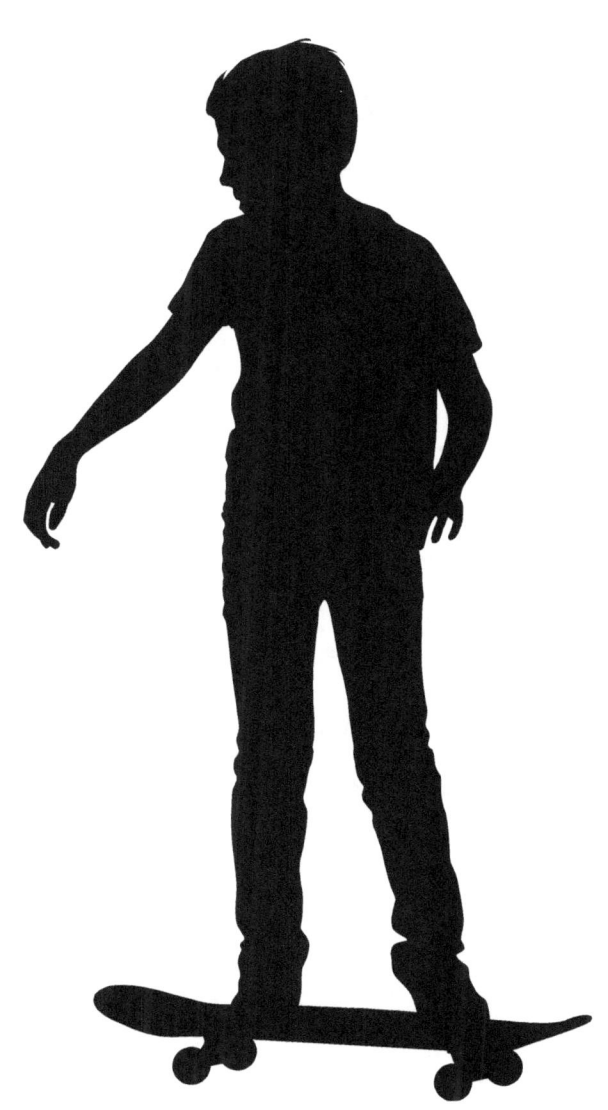

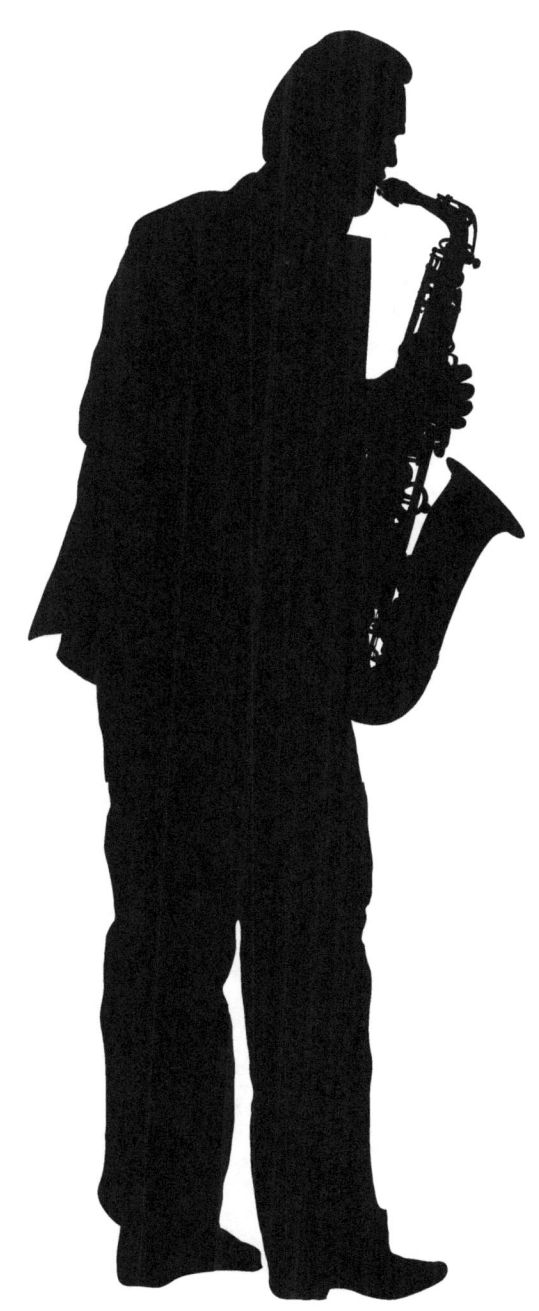

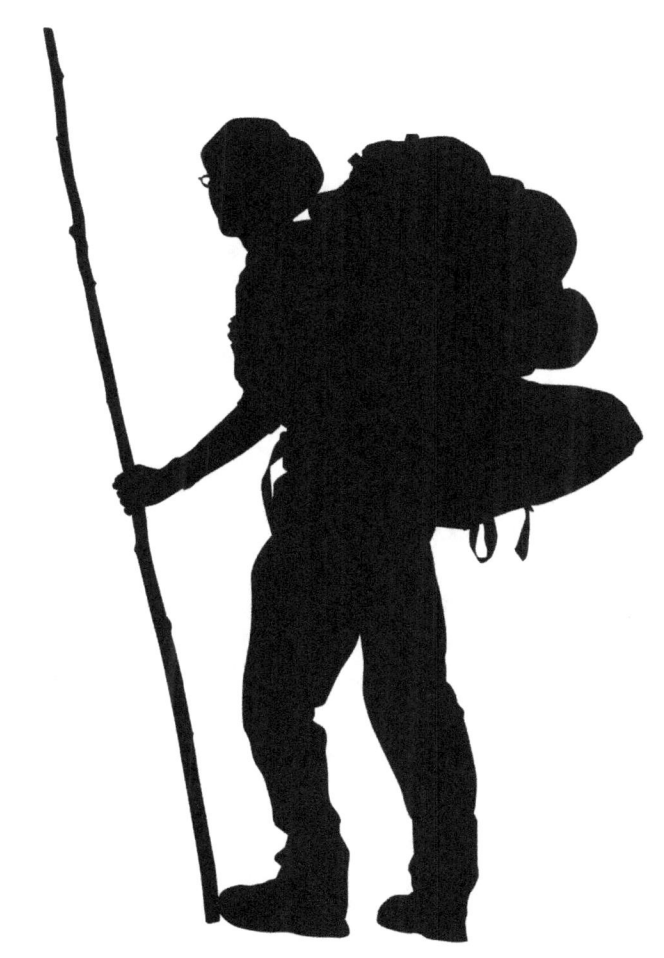

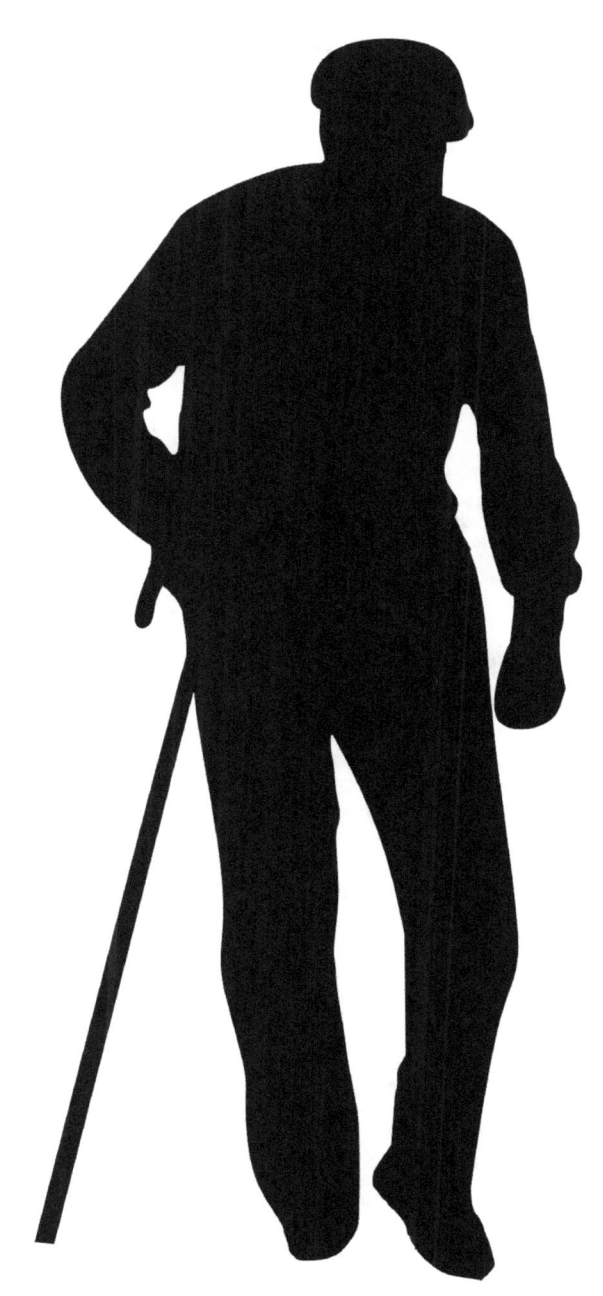

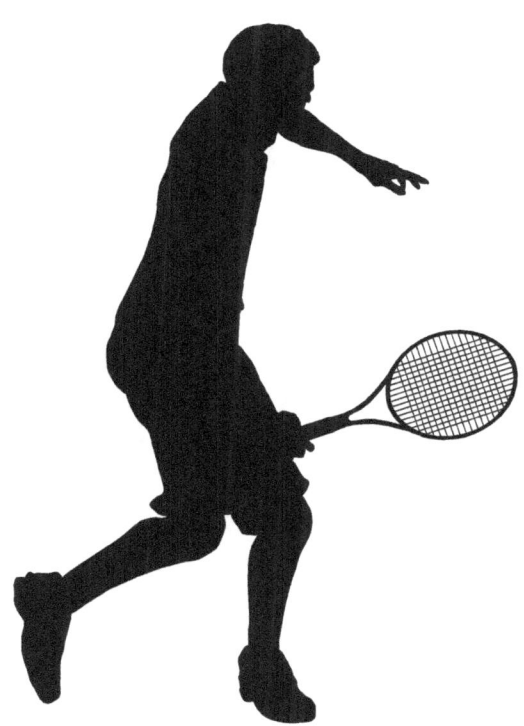

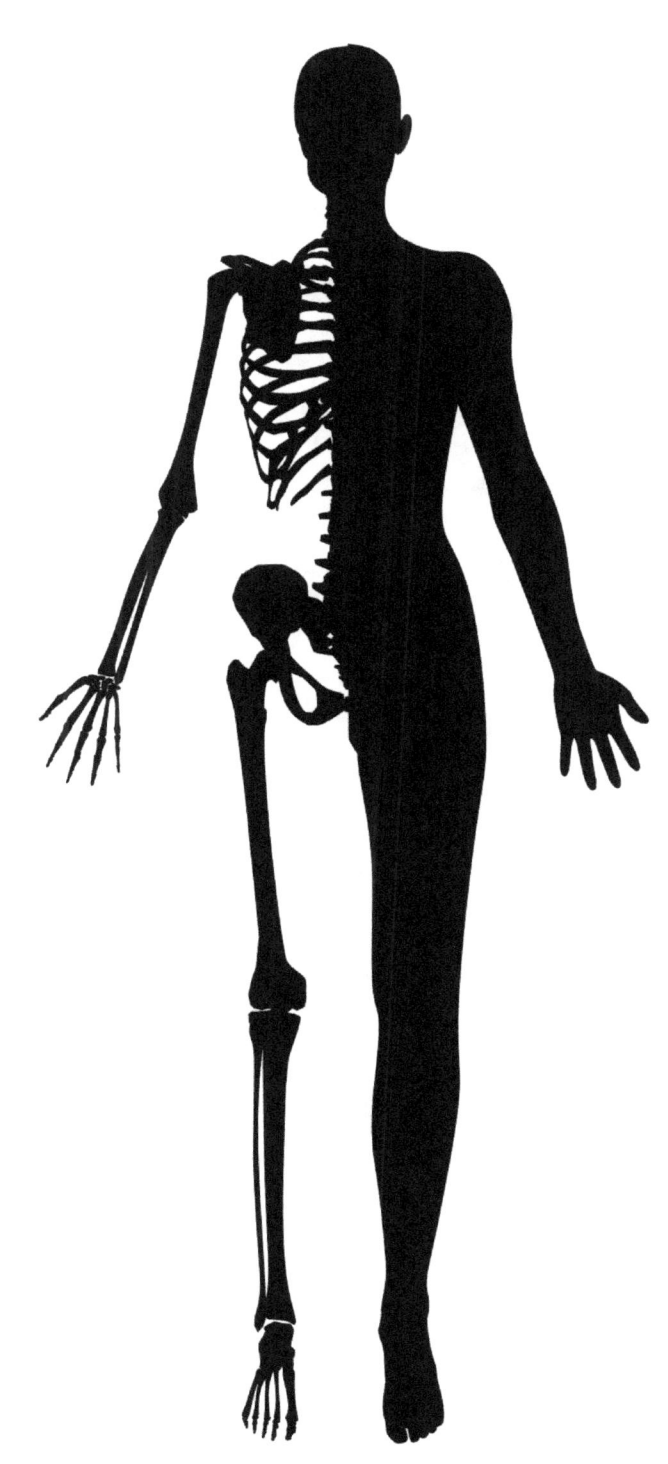

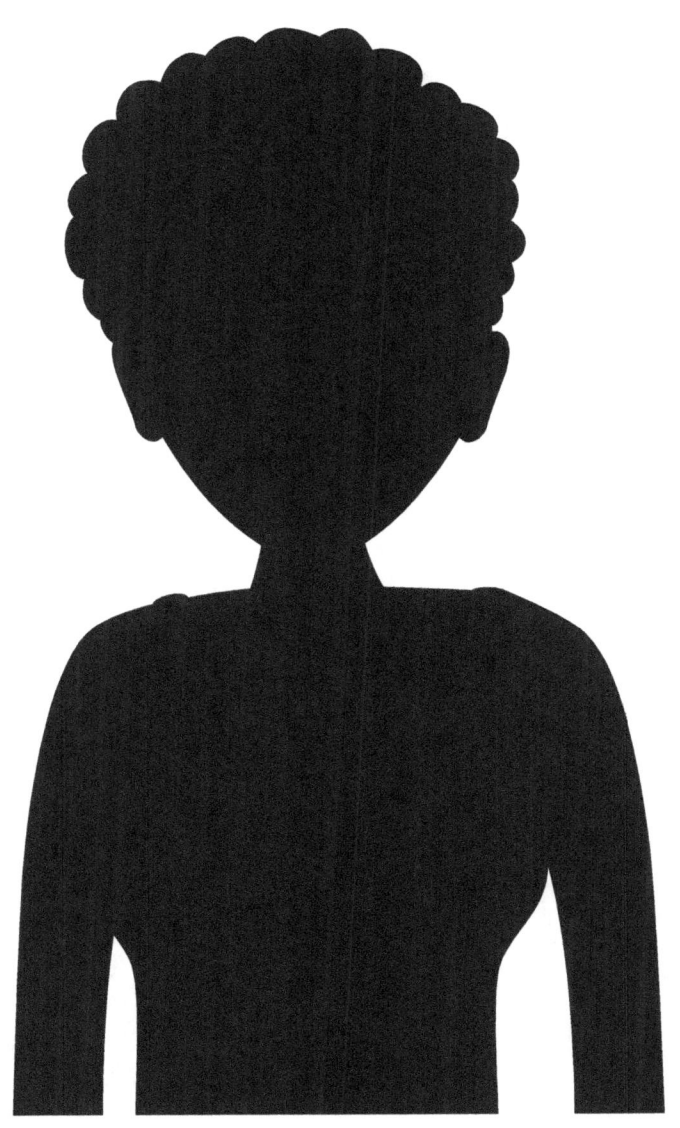

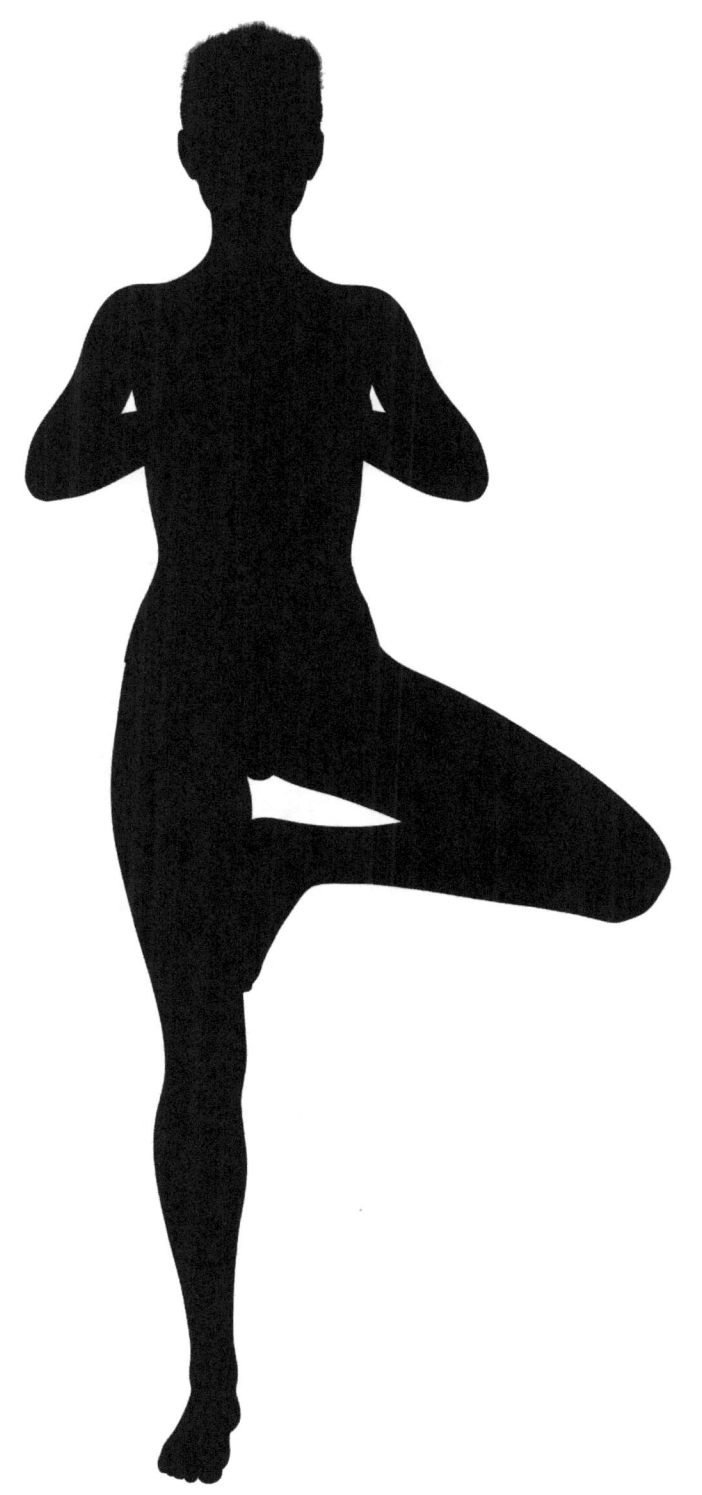

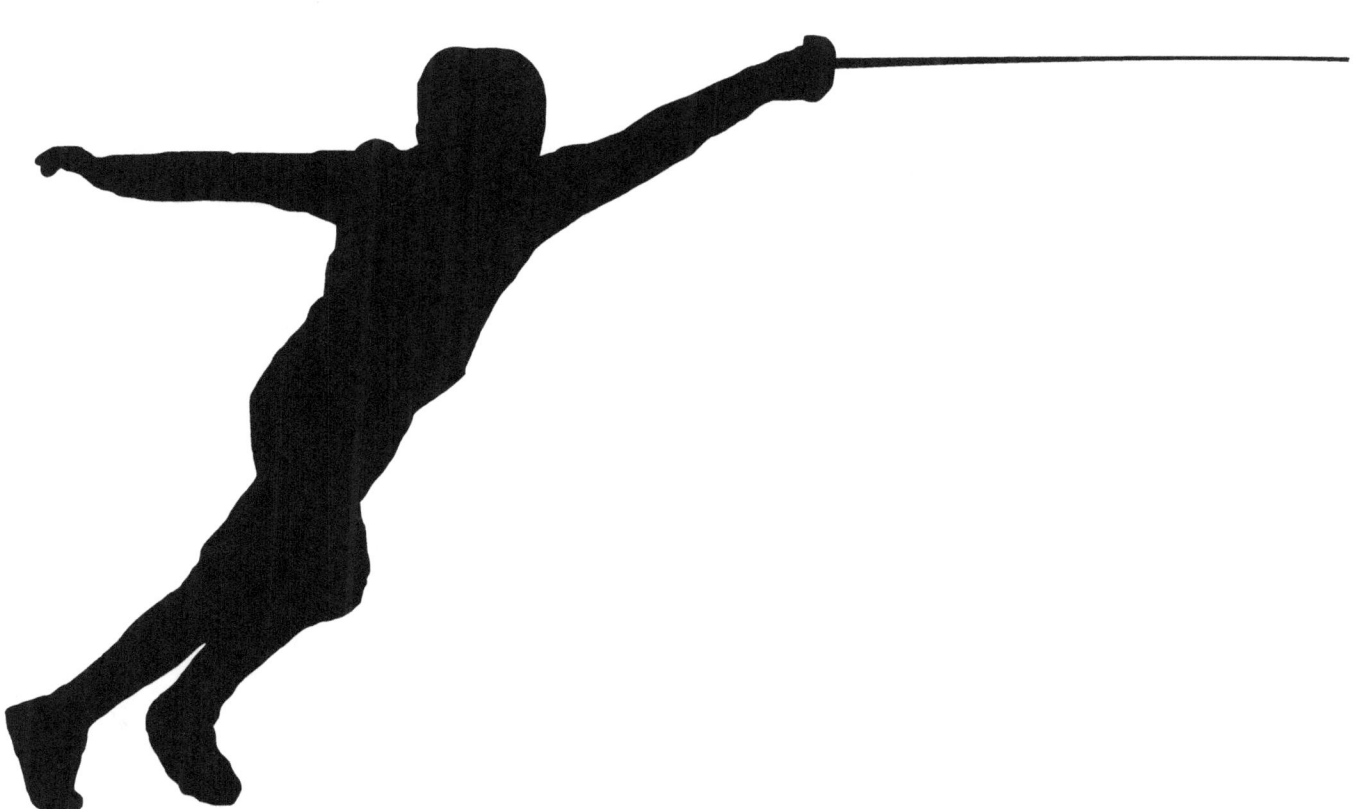

....

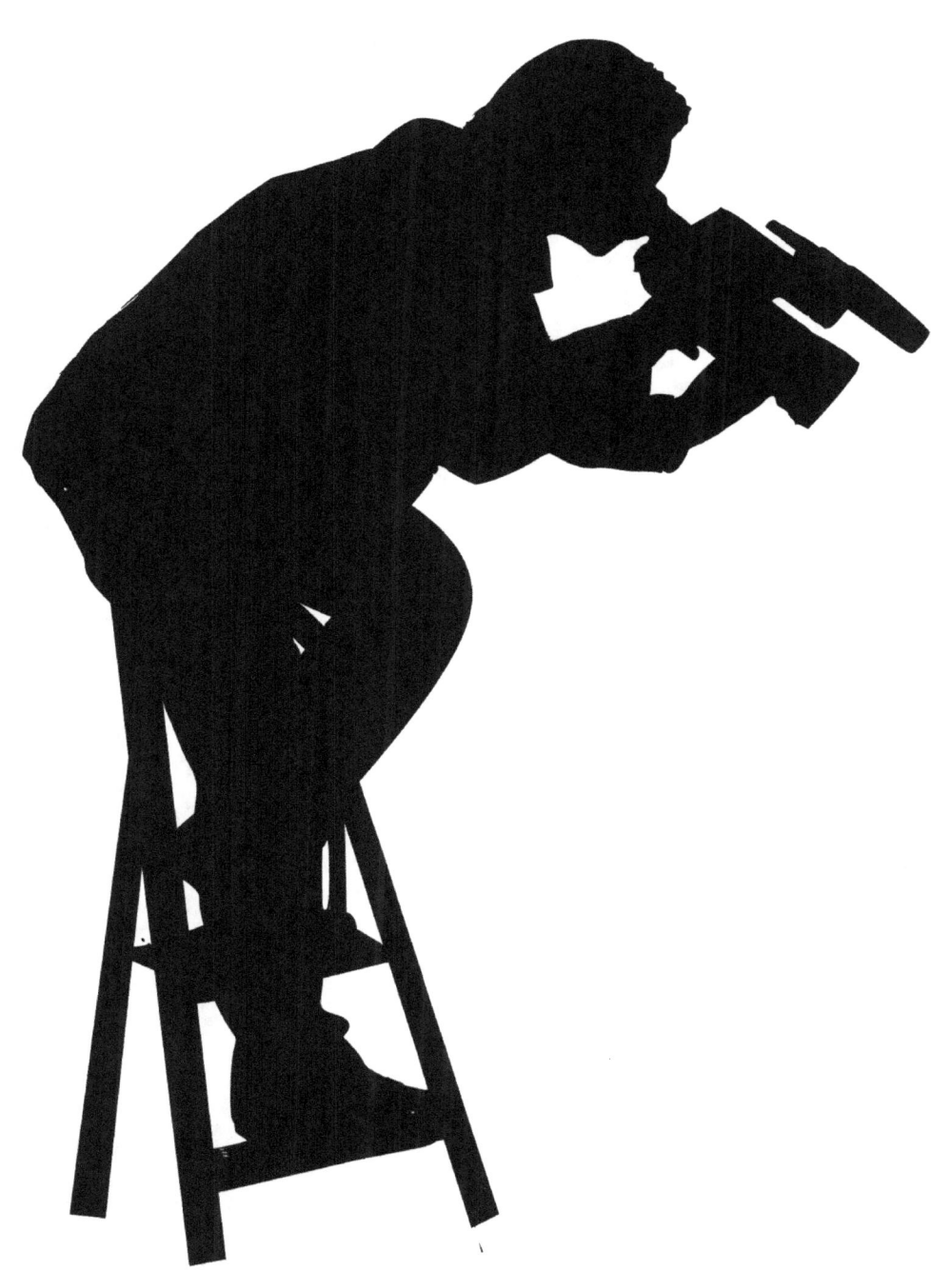

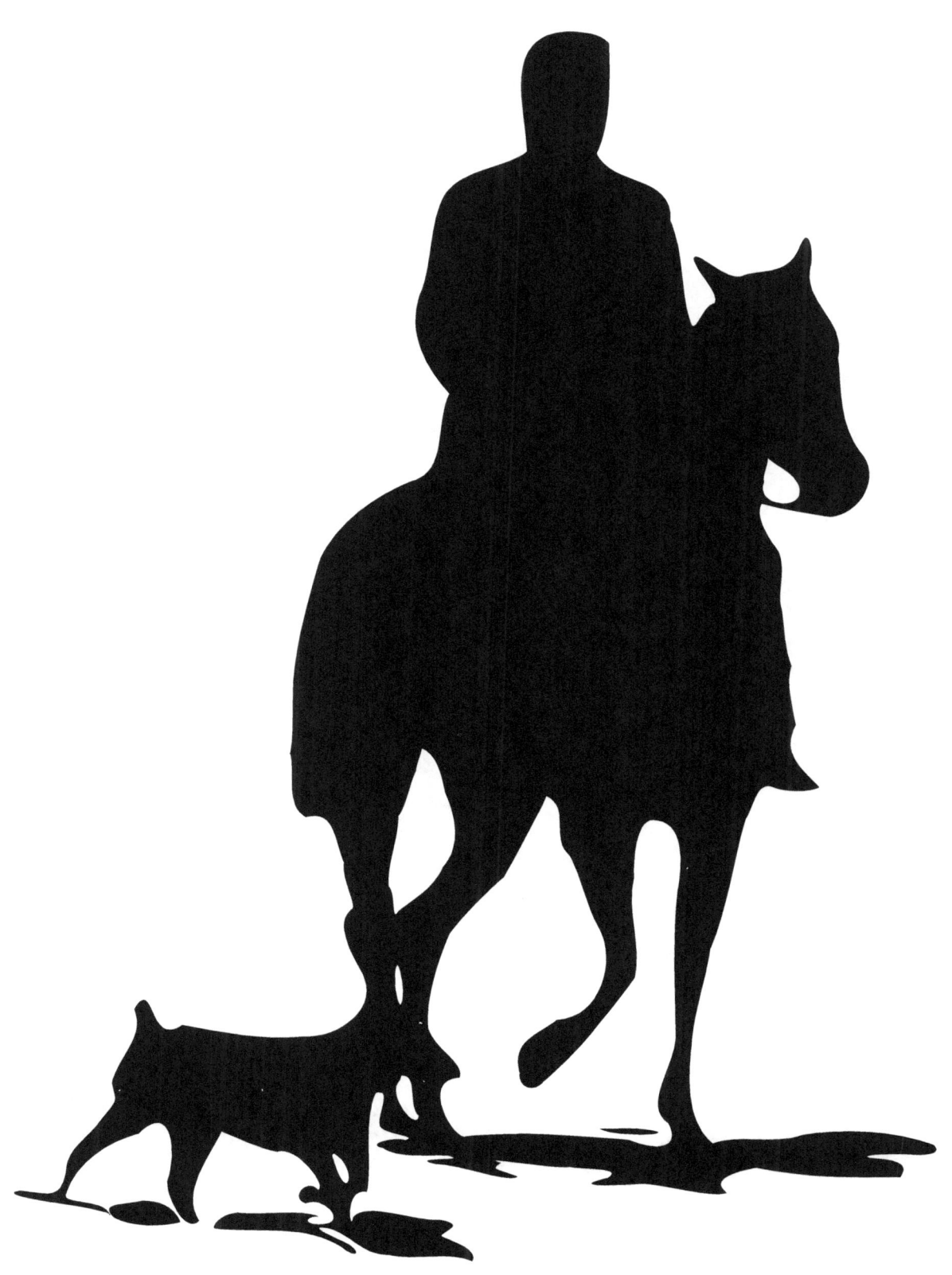

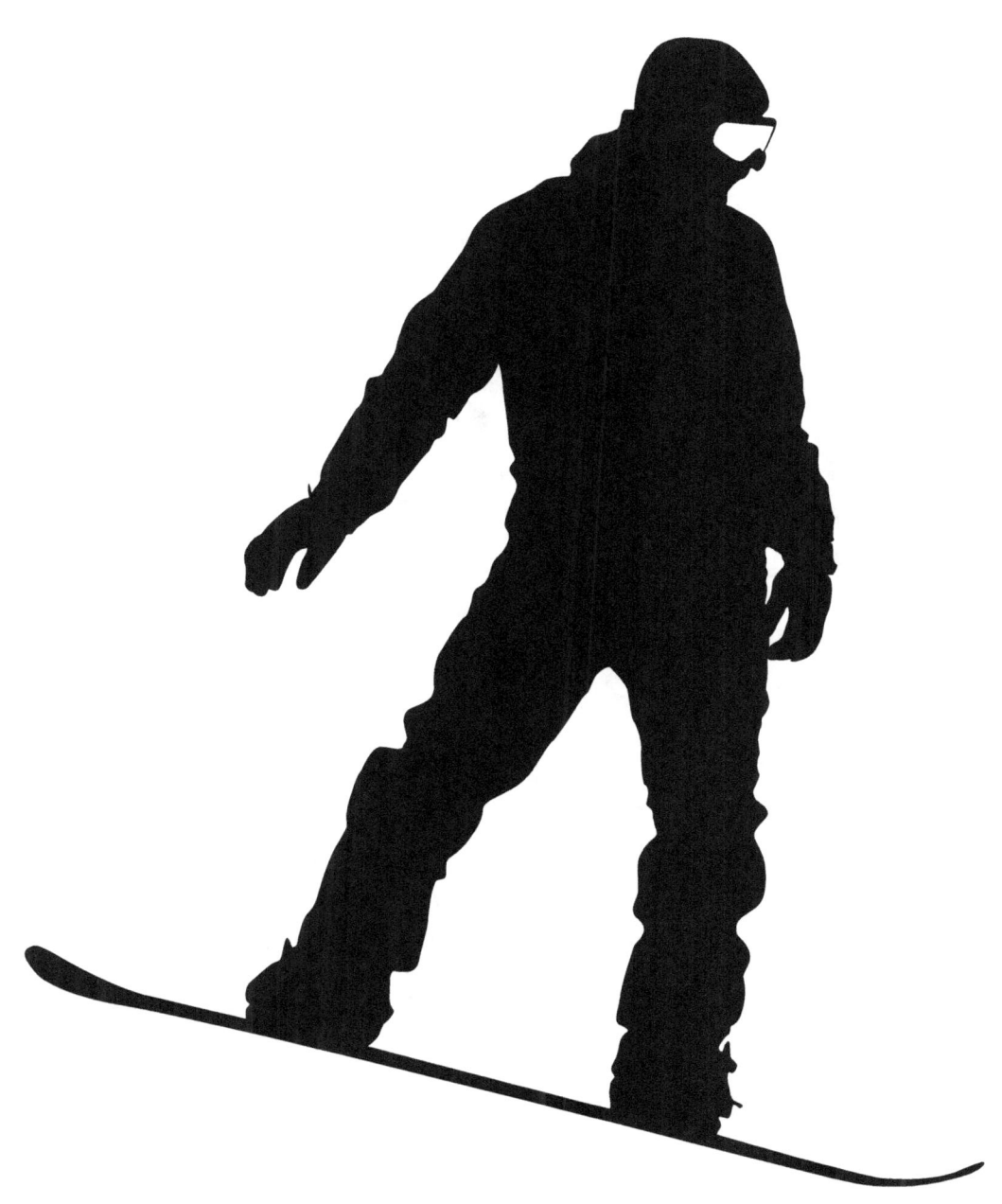

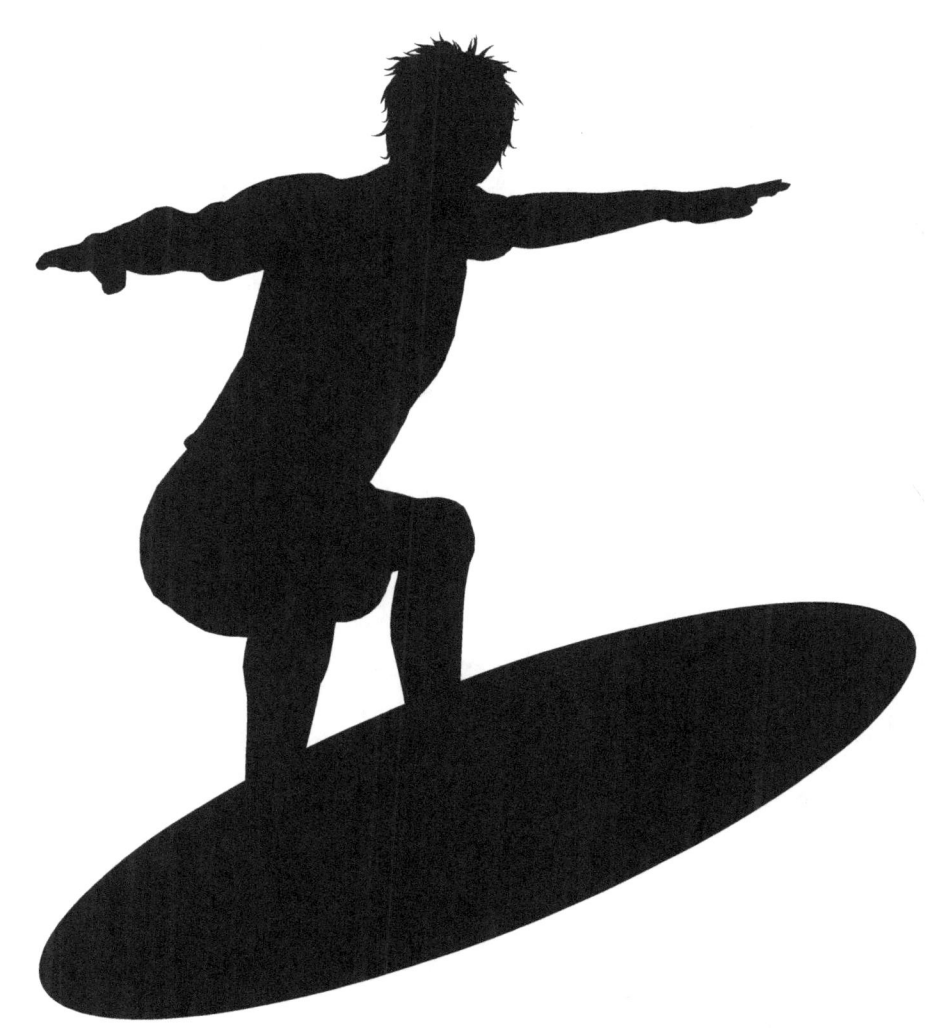

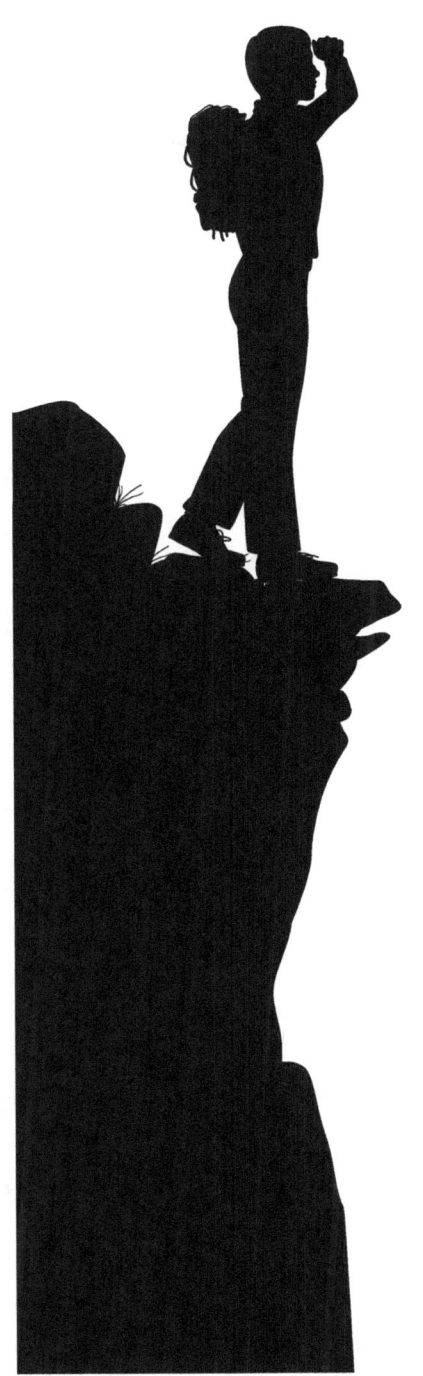

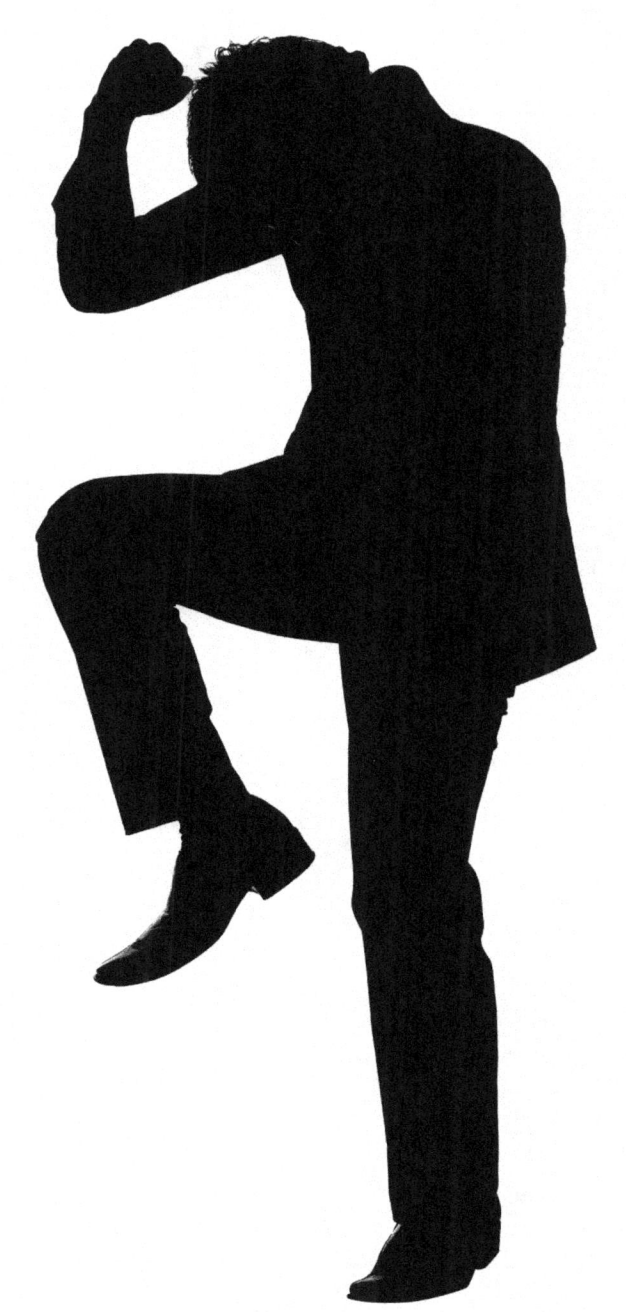

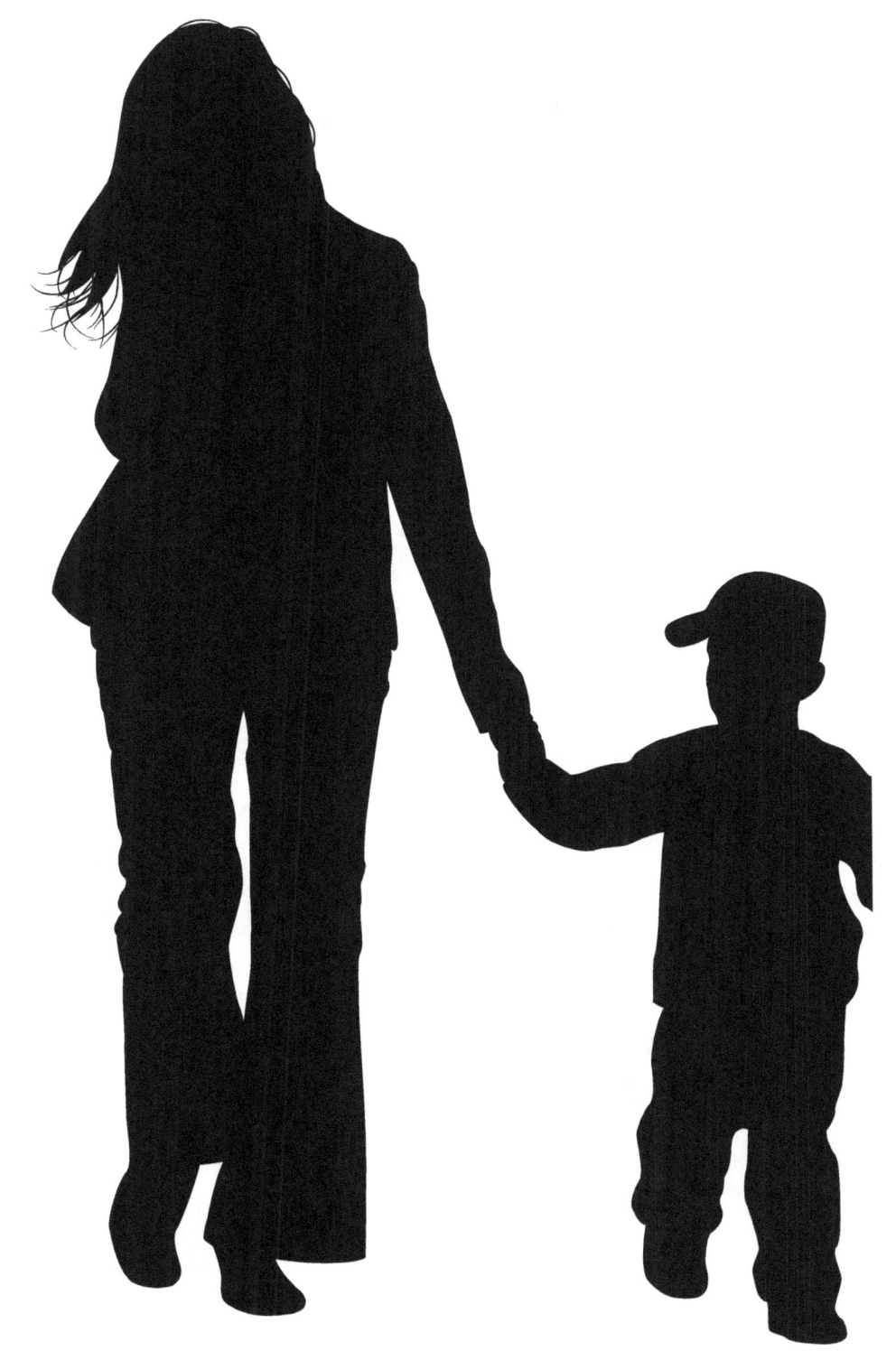

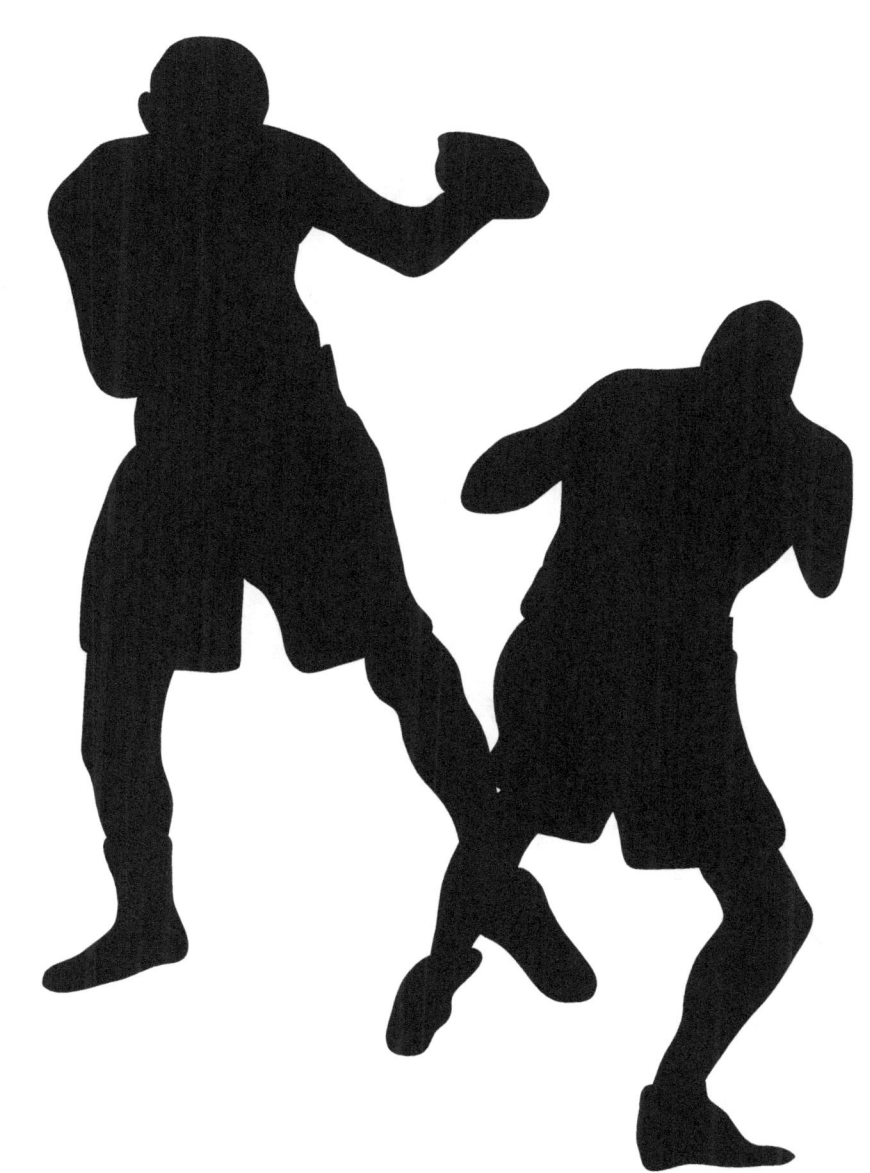

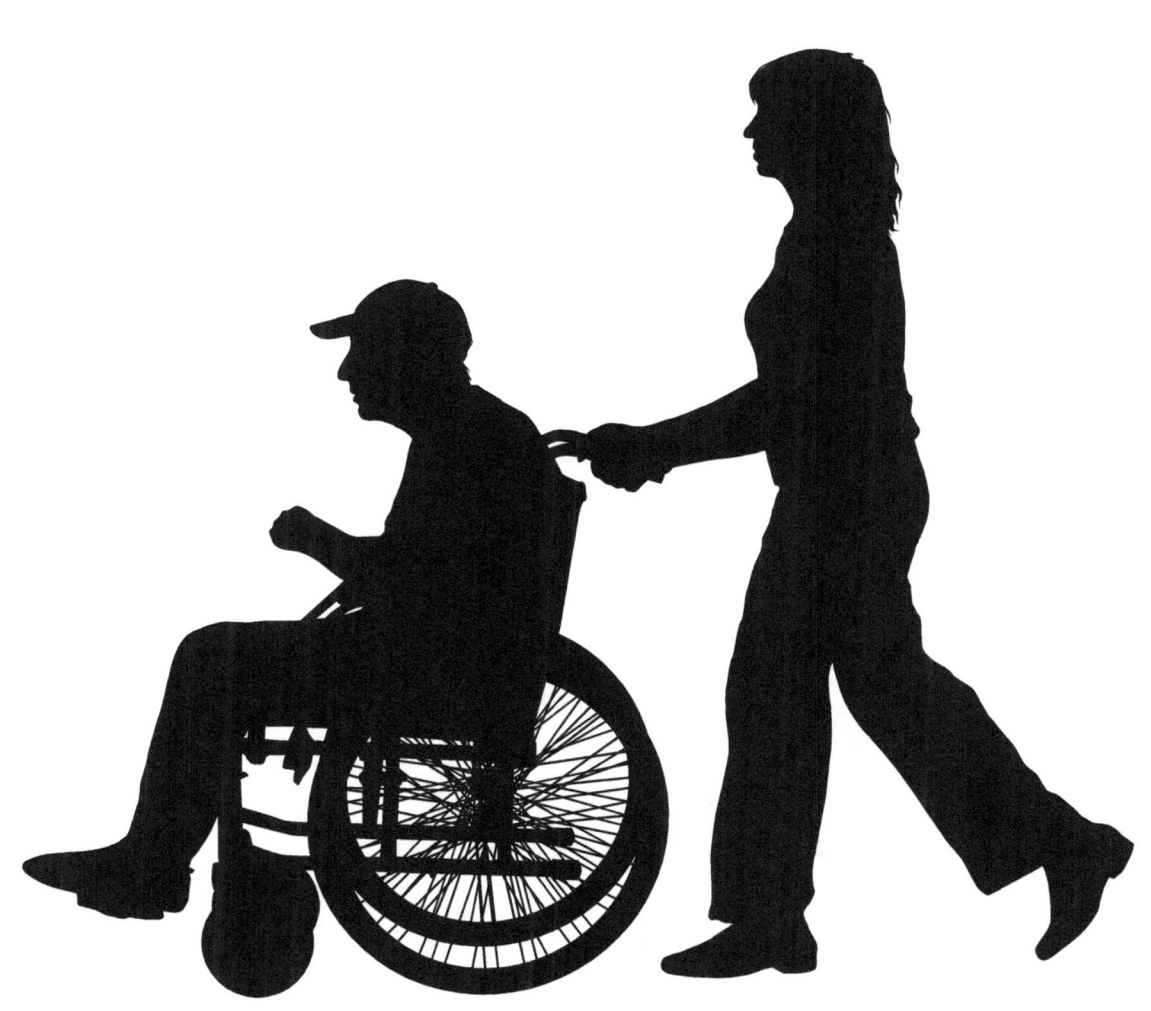

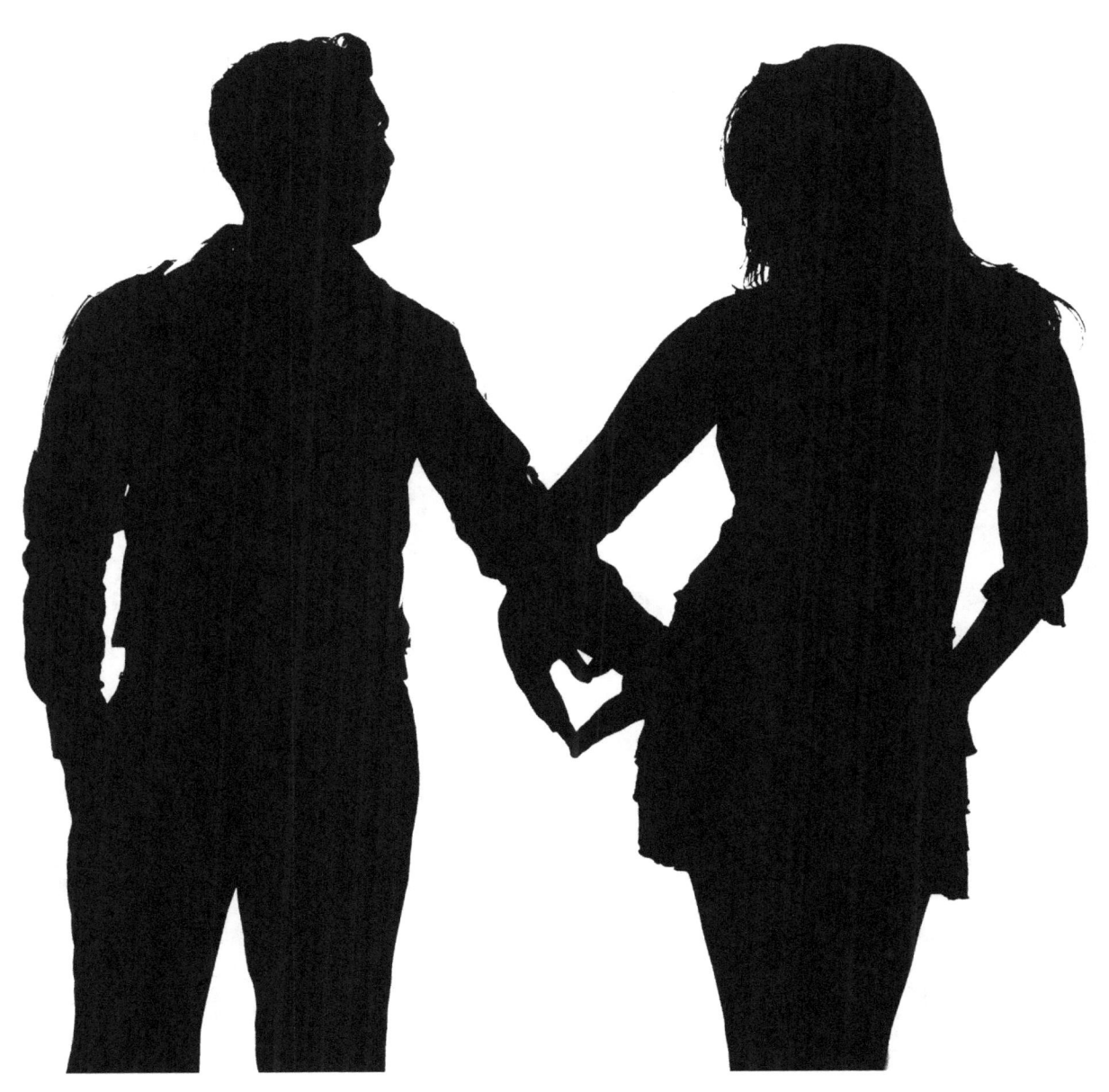

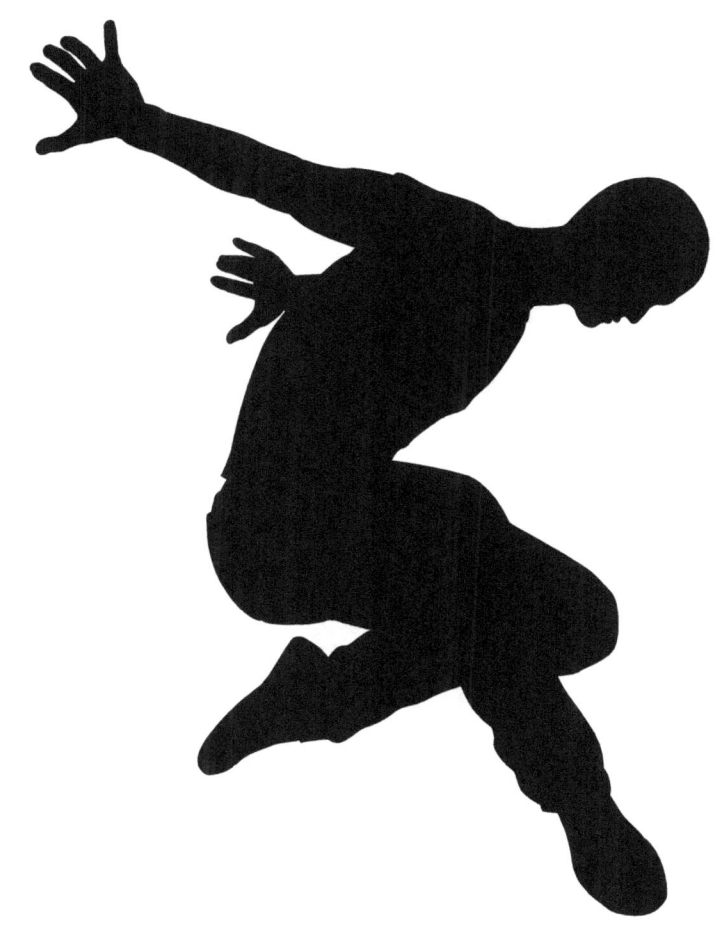

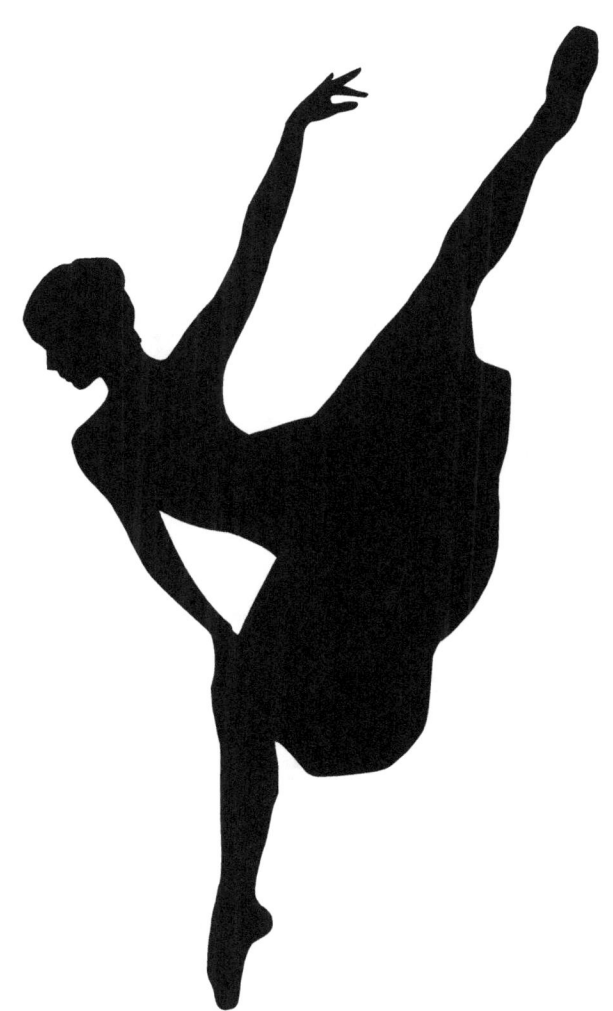

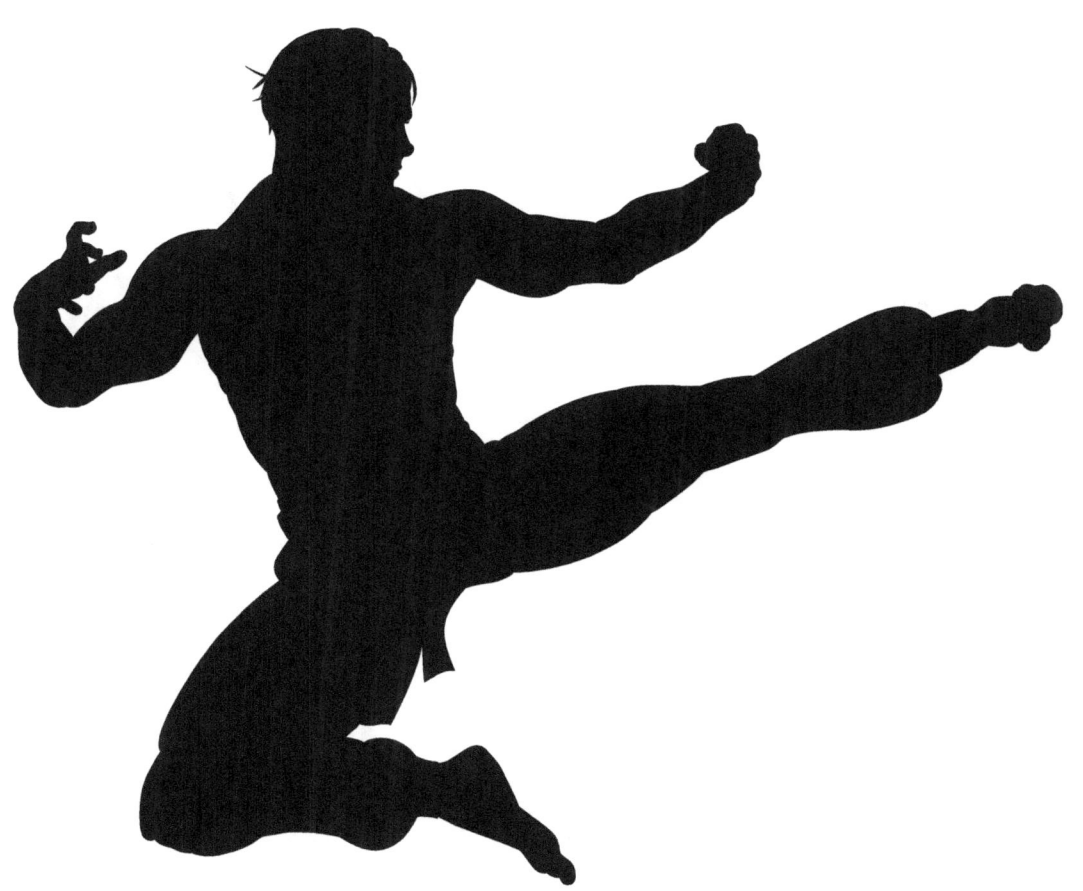

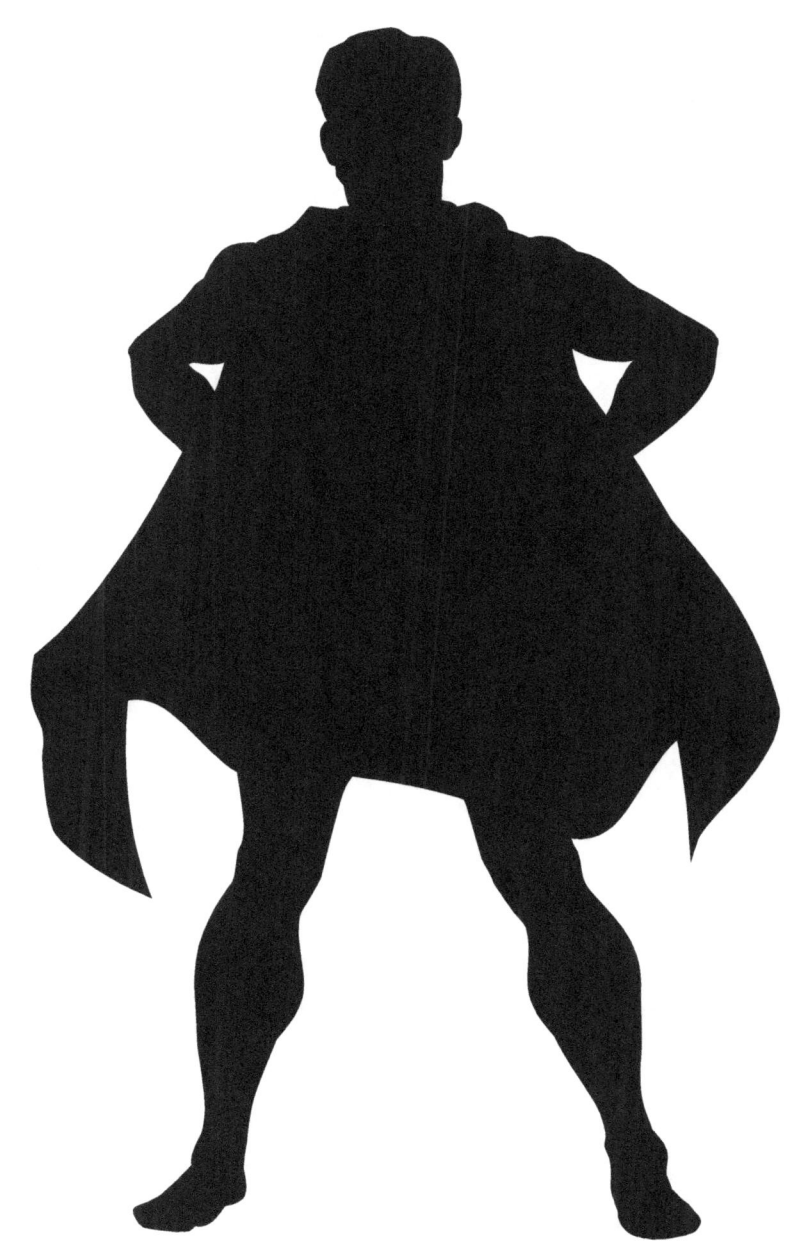

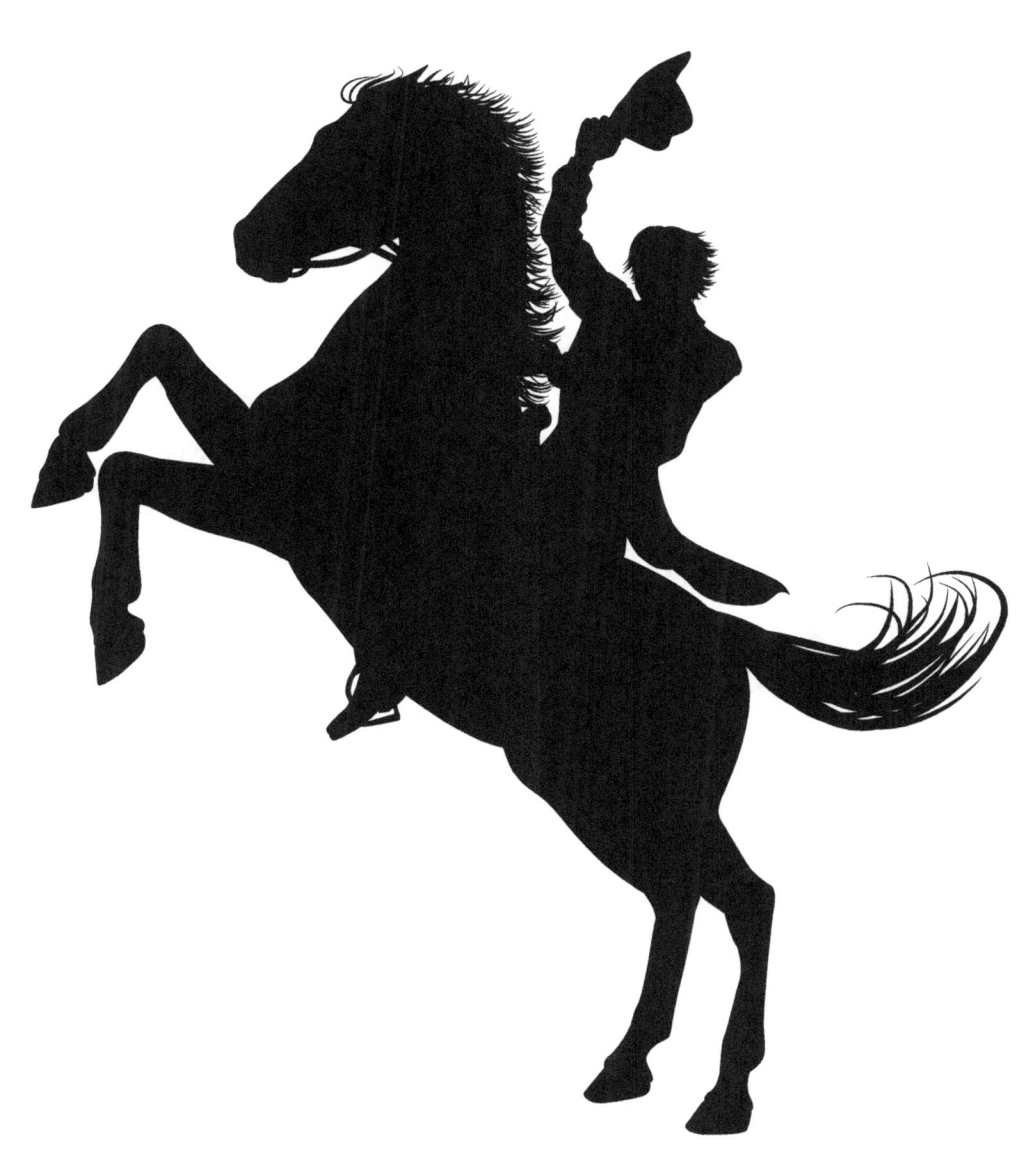

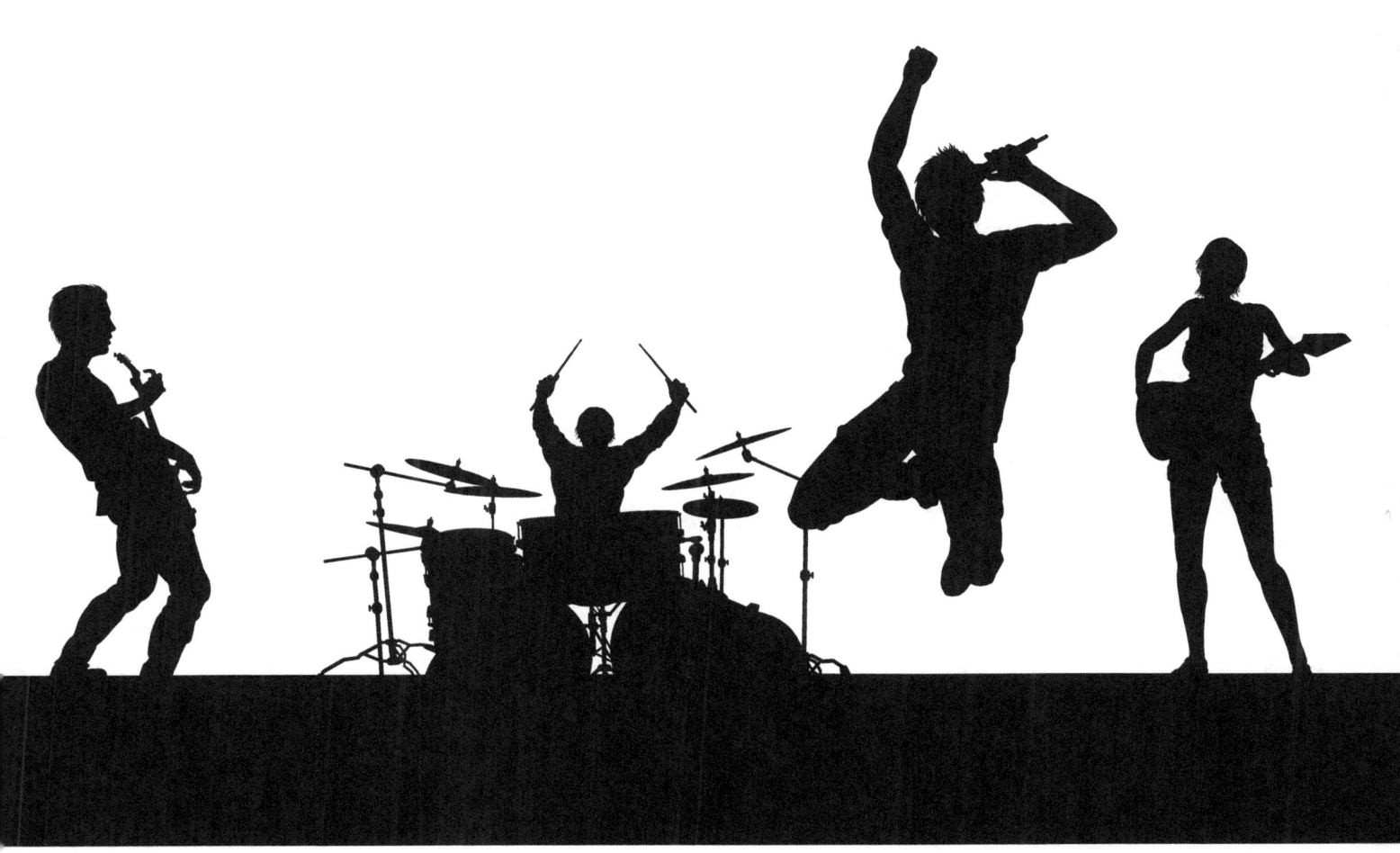

....

Hope you enjoyed your first silhouette book. The possibilities are endless with how you create them. Look for our new titles being released. Want a few free pages?

Send your email address to leslietimm4@gmail.com.

www.ingramcontent.com/pod-product-compliance
Lightning Source LLC
Chambersburg PA
CBHW080613220526

45466CB00010B/3329